The tale of Tortoise Buffett

13HABITS.COM

Start today.
Do it with a passion.
Make it a habit.
- Lucas Remmerswaal

The tale of Tortoise Buffett
Shareholder Letters by Warren Buffett: www.berkshirehathaway.com/letters/letters.html
Story and Creative Direction by Lucas Remmerswaal: www.lucasremmerswaal.com
Original Art and illustrations by Annette Lodge: www.annettelodge.com
Concept development layout and design by Karl Fountaine: www.fountainedesign.co.nz

Title: The tale of Tortoise Buffett
Author: Lucas Remmerswaal
Publisher: Lucas Remmerswaal
Address: 57 Crawford Cres, Kamo, Whangarei
LCCN: 2011904700

I met Warren Buffett at Piccolo Pete's,
one of his favorite restaurants in Omaha.
When I approached his table I said to him:
"I'm Lucas Remmerswaal from New Zealand.
I've spent the last nine months creating
6 books for children about your habits."

Buffett chuckled and said to me,
"I hope it's not my bad habits........."

Good habits once established are just as hard
to break as bad habits! Start by reading the
"13 Habits that made me Billions"
Read everyday and in just 23 days
reading will become one of your good habits.
- Lucas Remmerswaal

13 Habits that made me Billions

Inspired by Warren Buffett

Lucas Remmerswaal

Illustrated by Annette Lodge

Look out for
our next book
in the series...

13HABITS.COM

Once upon a time there was a tortoise named Buffett, who loved reading and thinking, and a hare called Trader Hare who liked to borrow money.

Tortoise Buffett→

←Trader Hare

One day they had an argument about who could make money grow fastest.

"I'll try
not to beat
you by
too much,
Tortoise
Buffett!"

"May the best
animal win..."

They agreed on a goal
and started off the race to
see who could make their
money grow the fastest.

Quick as a flash, Trader Hare shot off to the bank and borrowed some money, so he would have capital to invest.

Tortoise Buffett also wanted to invest. But his investment capital came from the income he made by working hard. Really hard.

He sold Coca-Cola & chewing gum door-to-door, delivered newspapers, recycled golf balls, sold magazine subscriptions, and put pinball machines in Barber shops.

He knew the way to win was by saving 10% of his income, and then wisely investing his savings.

As Trader Hare thought he was
well ahead
of the tortoise, he had a
great idea:

He found a wonderful shady tree with soft green grass underneath. The whispering wind told Trader Hare, "sleep, sleep!"

Tortoise Buffett, still saving 10% of his income and investing with a purpose, passed the tree with Trader Hare sleeping underneath it.

Trader Hare soon woke up with a start as he remembered he must repay the bank before he could finish the race!

But whilst he had been asleep,
the value of his investments had gone down.

Trader Hare did not have enough
money to pay back his loan!

The bank made Trader Hare
bankrupt just as he made a
dash for the finish line...

Debt is a four letter word and →
means a four word sentence -
Be Prepared for Trouble.

... only to find the triumphant tortoise waiting for him.

Finish Line

Tortoise Buffett
the champion!

The moral of the story

Slow and steady wins the race every time. Tortoises read. Hares do not. Hares have no time to read! Tortoises hate "debt" - hares love to scuttle to the bank to "borrow" money! That is because they are frantic by habit and are urged on by this habit to rush, rush, and rush!

Work hard, save 10% of your income. Then invest your savings wisely! Tortoises hate "debt" and always keep enough cash in the bank for six month's living expenses.

And remember...

...good habits are the
basic tools that will determine
whether you are
a **tortoise**
or a **hare** in life!

The Champion!
Slow and steady wins the
race every time.

How Warren Buffett became a Billionaire

His father called him "Fireball" — it must have been Warren's energy and enthusiasm! The first thing that Buffett's dad taught him was that the inner scorecard is much more important than the outer scorecard. His dad was a 100% inner scorecard guy. His father was a stockbroker. Buffett loved Saturday mornings when he was allowed to "mark the board" at his father's office. There was a shelf full of books. Buffett got into the habit of reading them, thinking and acting on the wisdom he discovered. Before starting out in business Buffett did his research collecting piles of soft drink bottle caps, which he sorted and counted before recording the numbers in a notebook. The numbers told him that Coca-Cola was the most popular soft drink. For his sixth birthday his dad gave him $20.00. That was just the beginning of his snowball. "My first business venture - was buying a six pack of Coke for 25 cents and selling each bottle for 5 cents." At Christmas he got a nickel-plated moneychanger from his aunt Alice. Buffett loved wearing it on his belt as it made him feel professional when he went around the neighborhood selling Coca-Cola and chewing gum. To make more money Buffett got up early each morning to deliver newspapers. He saved his money carefully.

By the age of nine he read and re-read "How to Win Friends and Influence People" by Dale Carnegie and he learned not to criticize condemn or complain. For his 10th Birthday, his dad took him on a trip to the east coast. Buffett was so excited! They went by train from Omaha, Nebraska, and he got to decide on the places to visit in New York City. When Buffett wanted to see the New York Stock Exchange he got to meet Sidney Weinberg. Buffett has never forgotten that first visit. It inspired him to get back to work with a passion. On his return to Omaha, Buffett found a book in the Benson Library called "A Thousand Ways to Make a Thousand Dollars", in other words 'a million dollars'. As soon as he opened the book he was immediately hooked. Inside the front cover there was a tiny man with an enormous pile of coins and on the first page it said "Opportunity knocks". It had taken Buffett five years of work to save up $120.00. Buffett wanted to make even more money by investing his savings in the stock market so he could compound his money and make it grow!

At age 11, together with his older sister Doris his first business partner, they bought three shares of Cities Service Preferred. That purchase cost them $114.75.

Buffett started out selling chewing gum and coca-cola door to door around the neighborhood, delivering newspapers, collecting waste paper and magazines for scrap, recycling used golf balls, working at a bakery, working as a clerk in his grandfather's grocery store, delivering groceries and shovelling snow. When Buffett was 12 his Dad was elected to congress, the family moved to Washington. There Buffett put ferocious energy into throwing three newspaper routes. All his effort was rewarded at the age of 13 when he got the opportunity to deliver The Washington Post, a morning paper, to a high class apartment complex, The Westchester — consisting of five buildings owned by Queen Wilhelmina of the Netherlands. Buffett started at 4.30am on a Sunday morning. The route included two other apartment buildings and a small route of single-family houses delivering hundreds of newspapers each day. Next he added a sideline business selling calendars and magazine subscriptions to his newspaper clients. After school he would deliver the Evening Star. By the age of 16 Buffett had accumulated more than $2,000 and he invested alongside his father in a hardware store, Builders Supply Co. Next Buffett bought himself a forty-acre farm that was worked by a tenant farmer in Thurston County, Nebraska. There was a business selling collectable stamps, a car-buffing enterprise and a pinball machine business. Buffett cleared old stocks of cornflakes, barbeques and dog biscuits. These were the first steps to becoming a Millionaire and later a Billionaire.

"I must have tried about 20 businesses by the time I graduated from high school. There's a study I've often quoted that shows that the best correlation with business success is the age at which you started your first business. The earlier, the better. I got half the investment capital I started with delivering newspapers."
Warren Buffett, Billionaire & Philanthropist.

Glossary

Borrow money You can borrow money from a bank to buy an automobile, house or to buy or start a business. The borrower is really renting the bank's money for a fee called interest. This means that you pay back more money than you borrowed and this is how banks make their money.

Capital describes how much you are worth. When you add up the cash you have at home plus the money you have in the bank plus the valuable things you own the sum total of all these added together is your capital. Your capital is the money you have and the money you could raise by selling the things you own.

Businesses like Coca-Cola need capital to begin or expand production. The term capital describes the total sum that is needed to produce your favorite soft drinks.

Day Trader People that habitually buy and sell on the same day are called day traders. Some of the most commonly day-traded financial investments are stocks, stock options and currencies.

Debt When you borrow money from a bank or a person it is called a debt. So a debt is simply when you owe money to someone else.

Family budget When your family decides to save money, the next step is to make a budget. A budget is a plan that estimates your income and expenses.

Your family should begin by estimating its total income per week or month then estimate its total expenses per week or month. To know how much you can save, take your income and minus your expenses, the amount left over is what your family will be able to save.

Home Loan Home buyers can rarely pay for the full cost of a house or home. Most must borrow a large part of the purchase price, pledging the house, lot and down payment as security to the bank. Pledging these things as security means if at some stage they are unable to pay back the loan, the bank can sell these things to get the money back.

Interest is a fee that is charged for borrowing money. It is usually a percentage of the amount you borrowed and is added to the total. So if you borrow $100 for 1 year and your interest is 10%, you will pay back $110.

Invest When you invest you are taking saving your money one step further. If you put your money into a business, this is called an investment. The money you have invested can help the business which can mean you make money or 'profit'. You invest with the hope of receiving a profit.

For short term investments you can invest your savings in the money market, corporate bonds and government notes.

For longer periods of time, say 5 to 10 years you can invest your savings in the share market. When you invest in stocks, they are businesses such as Coca-Cola that makes and sells your favorite drinks.

Loan When you want to buy or build a house and you do not have the large amount of money required to do so but you have saved enough money for the down payment, you may borrow the remainder of the money required to pay for the house from a bank.

Profit Profit is earned, when for example you buy a bottle of coke for $1 and sell it for $1.20 you have made a 20c profit.

Save One of the best things you can do with your money is save and invest it. When you save your money in a bank account the bank is then able to lend someone else money to buy a house or buy or start a business. This is how a bank makes money because the person who borrowed the money pays the bank back what they borrowed plus interest. If people don't save money, banks can't lend other people money and the economy wouldn't grow and flourish.

Thank You

To Warren Buffett for making his Shareholders letters freely available. To the students and teachers at Hurupaki Primary and Kamo Intermediate School in Whangarei who generously gave their time to support this project, to them I am truly grateful.

I am especially thankful to my wife Noela, my children, my father, my family, Annette Lodge, Prof. John Hattie, Karl Fountaine, and the team at Amazon.com.

Made in the USA
Lexington, KY
05 August 2013